GREAT LATERAL THINKING PUZZLES

Paul Sloane & Des MacHale
Illustrated by Myron Miller

 Sterling Publishing Co., Inc.   **New York**

Acknowledgments

We would like to thank GAMES magazine for allowing us to reproduce puzzles which first appeared in their "How Come" Competition in 1992. These puzzles are: The Elder Twin by Judy Dean, The Seven-Year Itch by Dee Bruder, The Book by Dan Crawford, The Plane Crash by Lori Lavalle, Mountains Ahead by Bob Loper, High Office by Dave O'Brien, and A Good Night's Sleep by Kristen Stowe. Pat Squires contributed the idea in Suitcase for Hire.

Edited by Claire Bazinet

Library of Congress Cataloging-in-Publication Data

Sloane, Paul.
    Great lateral thinking puzzles/Paul Sloane & Des MacHale.
        p.   cm.
    Includes index.
    ISBN 0-8069-0553-0
    1. Puzzles.   I. MacHale, Des.   II. Title.
GV1493.S593   1994
793.73—dc20   93-45395
                                                       CIP

10   9   8

Published by Sterling Publishing Company, Inc.
387 Park Avenue South, New York, N.Y. 10016
© 1994 by Paul Sloane & Des MacHale
Distributed in Canada by Sterling Publishing
% Canadian Manda Group, P.O. Box 920, Station U
Toronto, Ontario, Canada M8Z 5P9
Distributed in Great Britain and Europe by Cassell PLC
Villiers House, 41/47 Strand, London WC2N 5JE, England
Distributed in Australia by Capricorn Link (Australia) Pty Ltd.
P.O. Box 6651, Baulkham Hills, Business Centre, NSW 2153, Australia
Manufactured in the United States of America
All rights reserved

Sterling ISBN 0-8069-0553-0

CONTENTS

INTRODUCTION

Exercise is good for the brain. These puzzles form a sort of mental fitness course to stretch and develop your powers of lateral thinking. You may even get additional exercise when you hear the answers—if you kick yourself!

The puzzles consist of strange-sounding situations, often drawn from real life. Each has a perfectly good explanation. You have to figure out what it is. The Clues section provides hints when you are stumped. You will probably enjoy these puzzles more if you discuss them in a group rather than as a solitary reader. It is best if one person, knowing the solution, answers questions posed by the others in the group. Questions should be formed so that they can be answered either "yes," "no," or "irrelevant."

As you approach the puzzles, it is best to test all your assumptions. Ask broad questions to establish what is really happening in the situation. You will need to be logical and imaginative at the same time. When one line of questioning leads nowhere, you need to approach the problem from a fresh direction—that is what lateral thinking is all about.

The puzzles are arranged into four main groups with two WALLY Tests interspersed for light relief. The easier problems are in the Tempting Puzzles section and the most difficult ones come under Diabolical Puzzles. There is a section of Grisly Puzzles, all of which feature death, accident, or mutilation; these puzzles are among the most popular but they are not for the squeamish. The WALLY Tests are just for fun: they consist of trick questions deliberately designed to catch you out.

The world needs lateral thinkers, people who can bring a fresh approach to current problems in all walks of life. We need people who can develop imaginative new solutions. These puzzles are amusing diversions, but they may also help create a new legion of lateral thinkers.

THE PUZZLES

1 Tempting Puzzles

1.1 A Fishy Tale

A woman had a pet goldfish which she loved very dearly. One day she noticed that it was swimming feebly in its bowl and it looked very unwell. She rushed to the vet with her prized pet and he told her to come back in an hour. When she returned she found the goldfish swimming strongly and looking healthy again. How had the vet managed this?

1.2 The Lost Passenger

Little Billy was four years old and both his parents were dead. His guardian put him on a train to send him to a new home in the country. Billy could neither read nor write nor remember the address, so a large label on a string was secured around his neck clearly indicating Billy's name and destination. However, despite the best efforts and kindness of the railway staff, Billy never arrived at his new home. Why?

1.3 The Book

A woman walked up to a man behind a counter and handed him a book. He looked at it and said, "That will be four dollars." She paid the man and then walked out without the book. He saw her leave without it but did not call her back. How come?

1.4 A Hairy Problem

Why is it that, in general, the hair on a man's head goes grey before the hair in his moustache does?

1.5 The Birds

Two naturalists were walking in the country. They were both keen to protect the environment and to conserve nature and wildlife. One said to the other, "I was impressed by the way that you hit that bird." The second replied, "Yes, it was good, but not as good as that large bird that you hit earlier." What were they talking about?

1.6 Blinded at Teatime

A man was drinking a cup of tea when he was suddenly blinded. How?

1.7 Countdown

A man was slowly counting but unfortunately he miscounted. A little later he suffered a sharp pain in his back. Why?

1.8 Weather Forecast

John was watching television. Just after the midnight news there was a weather forecast: "It is raining now and will rain for the next two days. However, in 72 hours it will be bright and sunny." "Wrong again," snorted John. He was correct but how did he know?

1.9 No West

Let us agree that at the North Pole it is impossible to look north and at the South Pole it is impossible to look south. Then, where in the world would you be if you could look north and south but could not look east or west?

1.10 The Blind Beggar

A blind beggar had a brother who died. What relation was the blind beggar to the brother who died? ("Brother" is not the answer.)

1.11 The Truck Driver

A police officer saw a truck driver clearly going the wrong way down a one-way street, but did not try to stop him. Why not?

1.12 Mountains Ahead

You are seated next to the pilot of a small plane at an altitude of one mile. Huge mountains loom directly ahead. The pilot does not change speed, direction, or elevation, yet you survive. How come?

1.13 A Strange Christening

During a christening ceremony, the godmother of the child suddenly tackled the priest who was conducting the ceremony, knocked him down, and rolled him over on the ground. Why did she do this?

1.14 Pond Problem

A man wishes to reach the island in the middle of an ornamental lake without getting wet. The island is 20 feet from each edge of the pond (see diagram) and he has two planks each 17 feet long. How does he get across?

1.15 Walking and Running

There were two keen sportsmen. One evening at 6 P.M. one started walking at 4 miles per hour and the other started cycling at 12 miles per hour. After an hour each of them stopped. They then each ran for fifteen minutes at 8 miles per hour. They both started from the same place, A. They both kept heading in the same direction throughout and never changed course or rested during the entire 45 minutes. They both arrived at point B at the same time. How could this be and how far was it from A to B?

1.16 Church Bells I

A detective was lying in bed one Sunday morning listening to the local church bells ringing. Suddenly he realized that he was listening to a recording. How did he know?

1.17 Church Bells II

One night the vicar noticed that the old clock in the church tower struck 13 times at midnight. It did the same thing the following night so he had the mechanism investigated. It was found to be in perfect order, yet the clock struck 13 again that night. Why?

1.18 A Popular Book

When this book first came out it was read only by a handful of very rich people. Now almost everyone has a copy and reads it frequently. But you cannot buy it in a bookstore or borrow it from a library. What is it?

1.19 River Problem I

A man came to a river carrying a fox, a duck, and a bag of corn. There was a boat in which he could ferry one of the three items across the river at any one time. He could not leave the fox alone with the duck, nor the duck alone with the corn, so how did he get all three across?

1.20 River Problem II

This time the man reached the river with a fox, a duck, and a bag of corn, but this fox ate corn as well as ducks! There was the same boat as before in which he could take only one of the three with him. He could not leave the fox with either the corn or the duck, and, of course, the duck would gladly eat the corn if they were left together. How did he get all three across?

1.21 River Problem III

A man wishes to cross a wide, deep river, as shown in the diagram. There is no bridge, no boat, and he cannot swim. How does he get across?

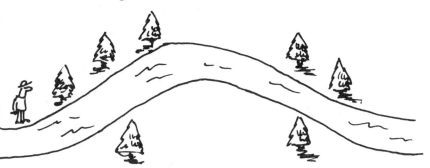

1.22 Bill and Ben

Bill and Ben are identical twins. They are physically very alike, fit and healthy. They are both good runners and always run at the same speed. Each runs against the clock on the same track under the same conditions. Yet Ben takes ten times longer to finish than Bill. Why?

1.23 The Missing Brick

Note: This puzzle and the one that follows it are products of the same cruel and devious mind.

A young couple were inspecting a house they were considering buying. In the middle of the kitchen floor they found a single brick. The real estate agent did not know why it was there, nor did the builder, so they sent for the architect. He took the brick outside and threw it up into the air, whereupon the brick vanished from sight. What was happening?

1.24 A Strange Flight

A small plane was flying from Albany to New York some years ago. Seated beside each other were a grumpy old man smoking a foul pipe and a grumpy old lady with a noisy pet duck on her lap. Each spent most of the journey complaining about the other. Finally a compromise was reached. The old man agreed to throw his pipe out of the window if the old lady would throw her duck out. This was done. Just as the plane was about to land, the lady was pleased to see the duck flying alongside the plane. What did the duck have in its mouth?

WALLY Test I

Back by popular demand, here is the latest World Association for Laughter, Learning, and Youth (WALLY) test. It consists of questions designed to catch you out. Be warned! Every low, nasty trick we can devise has been used. Get a pencil and paper. Write down the answer to each question as soon as possible after reading it. You have two minutes to complete the test, starting now:

1. What is twice the half of 1³⁄₇?

2. If two peacocks lay two eggs in two days, how many eggs can one peacock lay in four days?

3. How many cubic feet of earth are there in a hole measuring 3 feet wide by 4 feet long by 5 feet deep?

4. Do you know how long cows should be milked?

5. Where was Queen Cleopatra's temple?

6. In what month do Americans eat the least?

7. How many marbles can you put in an empty bag?

8. The greengrocer stands 6 feet tall, has a 46-inch chest, and wears size 12 shoes. What do you think he weighs?

9. If a duck came paddling down the Nile, where would it have come from?

10. How long will a seven-day grandfather clock run without winding?

See WALLY Test solution on page 20.

2 Intriguing Puzzles

2.1 Stamp Collection

A keen stamp collector who specialized in U.S. stamps saw an advertisement offering a complete set of early U.S. stamps for a fraction of what it was worth. He quickly bought it. Although it was a genuine, splendid collection and a real bargain, he was angry, not pleased. What was going on?

2.2 Sheepish Behavior

On a cold winter's day, drivers found that sheep from the fields nearby kept coming onto the road. There was no snow and the road was not warmer than the fields but whenever the sheep were ushered back to the fields they quickly returned to the road. Why?

2.3 The Tennis Match

Pete challenged Jim to a tennis match for a large bet. Jim won the first set easily (6–1). Pete then offered to raise the stakes to ten times the amount. Jim readily agreed but lost the next two sets to Pete 6–1, 6–1. Pete tried hard throughout the match and never threw away a point. How did he manage to suddenly beat Jim easily?

2.4 Surrounded

A man was on the run from the police. He was relaxing, watching a play in a crowded theatre. Suddenly he noticed that detectives were closing in on him from all directions and were covering all exits. How did he escape?

2.5 The Banker

Bernard was the president of a major Wall Street bank. One morning when he got on a crowded train he was extremely worried. When the train stopped and he alighted, he felt very sick but he was not worried anymore. Why not?

2.6 A Curious Place

If you liked this place you would rather stay for a day than a year, but if you hated it you would rather stay for a year than a day. Why?

2.7 Grandmother's Letter

A boy at boarding school ran short of money so he wrote to his grandmother asking for a small contribution. The response was a letter containing a lecture on the evils of extravagance but no money of any kind. Nevertheless, the boy was very pleased. Why?

2.8 Theft at the Wedding

During a wedding reception the father of the bride found that his wallet was missing. How did he find out who had taken it?

2.9 The Free Extension

A man went to a builder with plans for an extension to his house. They had never met before but the builder agreed to build the extension at no charge to the man. Why?

2.10 Bridge Crossing

In wartime, an army had to cross a wide river. There were no boats and only one bridge, which was very narrow. Crossing the bridge would have made them sitting ducks for enemy gunfire. How did the entire army cross the river in relative safety?

2.11 The Seven-Year Itch

While digging a garden, a woman unearthed a large metal box filled with money and jewelry. For seven years she

16

spent none of the money and told no one what she had found. Then she suddenly bought a new house, a new car, and a fur coat. How come?

2.12 Hit Out

A patient on the operating table is coming round after an operation. Suddenly he jumps up and strikes the surgeon as hard as he can. Why does he do this?

2.13 A Green Wedding

A clergyman was exasperated at having to sweep up vast amounts of confetti from the front of his church after every wedding. He decreed that in the future, if people insisted on throwing something at the married couple they throw something else. What did he suggest?

2.14 Sell the Truth

A manufacturer states that if middle-aged people told the truth more often he would sell a great deal more of his products. What does he manufacture?

2.15 The Dried Peas

In a sports shop there is a soccer ball containing a quantity of dried peas. Why are they there?

2.16 The Dog That Did Not Die

A mother told her six-year-old daughter that her pet dog had been hit by a car and killed. The little girl burst into tears. Half an hour later, the mother said that the dog was quite well and that it was all a mistake. Why did she do this?

2.17 High Office
. . . .

Tom cannot read or write or tie his shoes. He has never worked a day in his life. Despite these shortcomings, Tom is given an extremely important, prestigious, and well-paid job. How come?

2.18 The Follower
. . . .

A woman who was driving on her own pulled into a filling station and bought some gasoline. As she drove off she noticed a stranger in a car following her. She tried to shake him off by turning, accelerating, slowing down, etc. Finally she turned into a police station, but she was shocked to see him follow her in. He was not a policeman and there were no mechanical faults with her car. Why did he follow her?

2.19 Money to Burn
. . . .

A bank messenger, carrying a bag containing one thousand $100 bills, was robbed at gunpoint by a masked man. The man took the bag home and, without looking inside, he burnt it. Why?

2.20 Not a Kidnapper
. . . .

A banker was kidnapped and held tied up and blindfolded by a single kidnapper for several days. During this time he remained seated in a silent room and he never saw or heard his kidnapper. A ransom was paid and he was released. The police arrested a suspect who had a previous criminal record and had no alibi for the period of the crime. However, during questioning, the police inspector asked the suspect one thing and then released him. Why?

2.21. Ruination

In a factory in Buckinghamshire, England, in the nineteenth century, a bungling employee ruined an entire batch of the factory output. However, his employer was very pleased. Why?

2.22 The Bet

In the eighteenth century, long before the invention of the train or the motorcar, people delivered urgent messages using riders on horses. An English duke, a notorious gambler, once bet that he could have a letter delivered from one place to another 40 kilometers (about 25 miles) away in 45 minutes or less. This was much faster than a horse could travel. How did he win the bet?

WALLY Test I Answers

Here are the answers—get ready to kick yourself!

1. 1¾.
2. Peacocks do not lay eggs.
3. There is no earth in a hole.
4. The same way that short cows are milked.
5. On the side of her forehead.
6. February; it has fewer days.
7. One; after that it is not empty.
8. Apples, pears, potatoes, etc.
9. An egg.
10. Without winding it will run for no time at all.

Rate your score on the following scale:

Number Correct	Rating
8 to 10	Wally Whiz
6 to 7	Smart Alec
3 to 5	Wally
2 or less	Ultra Wally

2.23 Days Off

A man hired seven employees to work for him. After a few weeks he noticed that only six were ever at work on any day and that on each day a different one failed to show up for work. Why?

2.24 An Irish Puzzle

Chuck was an American on holiday in Ireland. His rental car broke down while he was in a little village and he was able to pull into a garage. There he asked how he could find someone to drive him back to Dublin. The man at the garage said, "I haven't been here long but I am sure that Milligan is your man. He lives in the big white house at the end of the village."

Chuck went up to the house and Milligan answered the door. "Can you drive me to Dublin?" asked Chuck. "No," answered Milligan and explained that in his old car he never drove outside the vicinity. However, as it was late he offered Chuck a room for the night. When Chuck awoke the next morning, he was shocked to see a huge golden eagle on the top of his wardrobe gazing down at him. Why did the man at the garage direct Chuck to Milligan?

3 Grisly Puzzles

3.1 A Shocking Discovery

A man met a beautiful woman in a bar. After a few drinks they agreed to go back to her apartment. In the morning he awoke in an alleyway having been drugged. He checked his wallet, watch and credit cards and found that none were missing. A few minutes later he discovered something which gave him a terrible shock. What was it?

3.2 Clean Sweep

A strong woman is about to start her cleaning job when she collapses in a faint. Why?

3.3 Death on the Boat

An expert sailor was killed while sailing his boat. He had suffered a heavy blow to the head. How had it happened?

3.4 A Rum Find

Two workmen were doing a major renovation job on an old English house. They could not believe their luck when they came upon a cask of excellent Jamaican rum. They indulged in a glass or two of this rum every day until finally it ran out. They then got a nasty surprise. What was it?

3.5 Broken Match

A man is found dead in a field. He is clutching a broken match. What happened?

3.6 The Cut Finger

A man is peeling potatoes when he cuts his finger. He immediately puts his hand into water and leaves it there for 30 seconds. However, when he pulls his hand out the cut has entirely disappeared. How can this have happened?

3.7 The Music Stopped

The music stopped. She died. Explain.

3.8 The Dog Choker

A woman came home to find her dog choking in the hall. She rushed the dog to a nearby vet and went home while he examined the dog. When she arrived home the phone was ringing. It was the vet warning her to get out of the house at once. Why?

3.9 The Movie

Tom and Joe went to a movie. There were many other people there. During a quiet scene, Tom drew a gun. Joe screamed, "Don't shoot!" but Tom shot him. Tom then left. Many people saw Tom leave and they restrained him. The police arrived and quickly released Tom. Why?

3.10 Damaged Car

A man was the proud owner of a beautiful and expensive

Mercedes sports car. One day he drove it to an isolated parking area and then smashed the window, scratched the doors, and ripped out the radio. Why?

3.11 The Motorcyclist

A man is lying severely injured in the road. He had quite deliberately stepped out from the sidewalk in front of a motorcyclist who had hit him. Why had the man done this?

3.12 Swimmer in the Forest

Deep in the forest, a forest ranger found the body of man dressed only in swimming trunks, snorkel, and facemask. The nearest lake was 8 miles away and the sea was 100 miles away. How did he die?

3.13 The Dark Room

A man walked into a small, dark room in a large building. After a few minutes he emerged from the dark room and left the building. A man then walked up to him and shot him dead. Why?

3.14 The Two Vans

In a bizarre accident, two identical vans simultaneously plunged over a dockside and into thirty feet of water. They both landed upright. Each van had a driver who was fit, uninjured by the fall, and conscious. One drowned but the other easily escaped. Why?

3.15 Suicide

A man wakes up in a dark room. He switches on the light. A few minutes later he shoots himself. Why?

3.16 The Plane Crash

Susan watched as her husband boarded the 8:15 P.M. Air Canada flight from Toronto to Chicago. She then drove home from the airport and proceeded to watch a movie. About one hour into the movie there was a news flash; the 8:15 P.M. Air Canada flight from Toronto to Chicago had crashed with no survivors. Susan did not react. She just continued to watch the movie. How come?

3.17 One Beautiful Morning

A man woke up on a beautiful summer morning. He went to the window, looked out in horror, and then shot himself. Why?

3.18 The Blanket Mystery

A man walked up a hill carrying a blanket. Because of this, one hundred people died. How?

3.19 The Deadly Bite

A woman gave a man something to eat. It caused him to die. It was not poisoned or poisonous. Why did he die?

3.20 Bad Boy

A man sitting at home was killed by a little boy who was outside. How?

WALLY Test II

Just when you thought you were safe—another WALLY test! As before, get a pencil and paper. Write down the answer to each question as soon as possible after reading it. You have two minutes to complete the test, starting now:

1. If a ton of coal costs $30 and a ton of coke costs $25, what will a ton of firewood come to?

2. Removing an appendix is called an appendectomy, removing tonsils is called a tonsillectomy. What is it called when they remove a growth from your head?

3. Why are U.S. soldiers forbidden to carry rifles any longer?

4. What three things that you can eat can you never have for breakfast?

5. If a farmer raises wheat in dry weather, what does he raise in wet weather?

6. What would you call a person who did not have all his fingers on one hand?

7. Which is greater, six dozen dozen or half a dozen dozen?

8. What is the best way to get down from a camel?

9. How could a man be severely injured by being hit by some tomatoes?

10. Why do Chinese men eat more rice than Japanese men?

See WALLY Test solution on page 35.

4 Diabolical Puzzles

4.1 The Nursery Rhyme

A man is visiting a young couple who have a one-year-old daughter. He takes the baby on his knee and, with the parents present, begins to recite a nursery rhyme with the child. Within a few moments, however, he is cringing with embarrassment. Why?

4.2 The Elder Twin

One day, Kerry celebrated her birthday. Two days later, her older twin brother, Terry, celebrated his birthday. How come?

4.3 Fair Shares

To divide a cake equally between two people you let one cut and the other choose. How could you divide a cake among three or more people fairly? No protractors, rulers, or measuring devices are involved, just a knife.

4.4 The Sealed Envelope

One morning a jealous wife found in the mail a letter addressed to her husband. How did she remove the letter from the sealed envelope without breaking the seal or tearing the envelope and then put it back in the envelope so that her husband did not know that the letter had been read?

4.5 Tattoo

Why did a significant number of people have a Crucifixion scene tattooed on their bodies? These people did not share any particular religious beliefs.

4.6 Suitcase for Hire

Pat went into a luggage shop to buy a suitcase. The assistant said, "It is most unusual to buy a suitcase. Why don't you rent one like all our other customers?" Why should this be so?

4.7 The Tennis Tournament

A total of 213 people enter a knockout tennis tournament. What is the least number of matches that must be played to decide an overall winner?

4.8 The Key

Every night before he went to bed, a man carefully locked all the doors of his house. Then he placed the front-door key inside a bucket of cold water. In the morning he retrieved the key from the bucket in order to open the door. Why did he do this?

4.9 That's Fast!

While Harry was working in his garage he made something travel at over 3000 miles (4800 kilometers) per hour. What on earth was it?

4.10 A Man in a Bar

A man walked into a bar and asked for a certain drink. The bartender apologized that he had run out of that particular drink but he offered the man any other drink in the house free. The man refused and walked out. Why?

4.11 The 88 Hours

A man sat perfectly still for 88 hours. Why?

4.12 Sand Trap

Why did a man go to great trouble to bury in the desert fifteen brand-new Mercedes-Benz cars, all greased and wrapped in plastic?

4.13 Building Demolition

In Australia a perfectly good building was demolished and an almost identical one erected on exactly the same site. The original building was in good condition, it had no defects and there was no issue of safety or planning permission. Why was it demolished?

4.14 The Torn Cheque

A man writes a cheque, signs it, and then tears it into exactly 217 pieces. He then puts it in the mail. Can you give a rational explanation for his behavior?

4.15 The Weather Report

A terse weather report once stated that the temperature in a certain place at midnight on June 1st was a certain number of degrees. Where was the place?

4.16 Odd Animals

What do these animals have in common: koala bear, prairie dog, firefly, silkworm, jackrabbit, guinea pig?

4.17 The Shorter Program

A music program on a well-respected radio station finished exactly eight minutes earlier than it was scheduled to. An embarrassed official gave the explanation for this mistake. What was it? How long was the program supposed to last? (It is possible to work this out.)

4.18 Traffic Trouble

How did a change in state traffic regulations lead to an increase in trade for local sex shops? (The answer is not obscene!)

4.19 Blackmail

A rather nasty criminal developed a seemingly foolproof way of extracting money from bereaved families. He would scan the obituary columns in order to choose the name of a wealthy man who had recently died. Then he sent an invoice for pornographic books addressed to the man and claiming payment for goods previously despatched. To avoid any scandal the family would invariably pay. How was he eventually caught out?

4.20 A Good Night's Sleep

A man in a hotel was unable to sleep. He got up, opened the window drapes, went back to bed and fell asleep easily. How come?

4.21 Grateful for Poor Service

A man saw something advertised at a certain price and went to buy it. An official refused to sell it to him even though the man could pay and other men and women were sold it. Later the man was very glad that his purchase had been refused. Why was he refused and why was he glad?

4.22 Free T-shirts

A man was watching television when he saw an advertisement offering free T-shirts to the first 100 viewers who phoned in. He called the number given, stated his size, and received his free T-shirt in a few days. Later he very much regretted doing this. Why?

4.23 Bank Robbery I

A gang robbed a bank. They tied up the staff and then hurriedly left the bank. One of the bank staff struggled free and did something which quickly led to the apprehension of the gang. What was it?

4.24 Bank Robbery II

A gang stole a bank security van containing over $700,000. Their plan was executed perfectly and they got clean away. The police had no trace of them and the gang were free to divide and spend the loot. However, they were extremely frustrated. Why?

4.25 A Puzzling Attack

Four rational and reasonable people were seated around a table. Suddenly three of them jumped up and viciously beat the fourth one senseless. Why?

WALLY Test II Answers

More answers—more groans!

10. There are more of them.

9. They were tinned tomatoes.

8. You cannot get down from a camel. You get down from a duck.

7. Six dozen dozen; it is 12 times as much as half a dozen dozen.

6. Normal; your fingers should be equally spread over two hands.

5. An umbrella.

4. Lunch, dinner, and supper.

3. The rifles are long enough already.

2. A haircut.

1. Ashes.

Rate your score on the following scale:

Number Correct	Rating
8 to 10	Wally Whiz
6 to 7	Smart Alec
3 to 5	Wally
2 or less	Ultra Wally

THE CLUES

1 Tempting Puzzles

1.1 A Fishy Tale

Q: Did the vet change the water?
A: No.

Q: Did he give the fish any medication, food, or tonic?
A: No.

Q: Had the woman had the goldfish for a long time?
A: Yes.

1.2 The Lost Passenger

Q: Did someone deliberately harm or abduct Billy?
A: No.

Q: Was his label removed in some way?
A: Yes.

Q: Was Billy a little boy?
A: No.

Q: Did Billy destroy the name tag?
A: Yes. (He ate it!)

1.3 The Book

Q: Was he surprised that she left without the book?
A: No.

Q: Did she pay the money to buy the book?
A: No.

Q: When she gave him the money, did she receive something in return?
A: No, not really, but she was quite happy to pay it.

1.4 A Hairy Problem

Q: Is this to do with the way the hair is cut, brushed, washed, or treated in any way?
A: No.

Q: Is it to do with eating, drinking, thinking, or talking?
A: No.

Q: Is it to do with timing?
A: Yes.

1.5 The Birds

Q: Had they each physically hit something?
A: Yes.

Q: Had they hit living or dead creatures?
A: No, neither.

Q: Had one of them hit an eagle?

A: Yes.

1.6 Blinded at Teatime

Q: Was there a flash of light or some other external occurrence?
A: No.

Q: Was the man physically normal?
A: Yes.

Q: Did something go into his eye?
A: Yes.

Q: Did this go into his eye because he was drinking the cup of tea?
A: Yes.

1.7 Countdown

Q: Was he counting as part of a task he was performing?
A: Yes.

Q: Was anyone else involved?
A: No.

Q: Would this happen to a woman?
A: Probably not.

Q: Was the pain caused by a pointed metal object?
A: Yes.

1.8   Weather Forecast

Q: Was John some kind of weather expert?
A: No.

Q: Did he have some special knowledge or insight into the future?
A: No.

Q: Is this to do with timing?
A: Yes.

1.9   No West

Q: Is there a place where it would be impossible to look east or west?
A: Yes.

Q: Is this because east and west are meaningless terms at this place?
A: Yes.

Q: Has anyone ever been there?
A: No.

1.10   The Blind Beggar

Q: Were the blind beggar and the brother both humans?
A: Yes.

Q: Did the brother and the beggar have the same parents?
A: Yes.

Q: Were they brothers?
A: No.

1.11   The Truck Driver

Q: Did the police officer and the truck driver both know that it was against the law to drive the wrong way down a one-way street?
A: Yes.

Q: Was there some emergency which justified either of their actions?
A: No.

Q: Should the policeman have taken action?
A: No.

Q: Was the truck driver committing a violation?
A: No.

1.12   Mountains Ahead

Q: Does the pilot have control of the aircraft throughout?
A: Yes.

Q: Is there a tunnel or hole or other way through the mountains?
A: No.

Q: Were you at any time in serious danger?
A: No.

Q: Did you fly over, around, or past the mountains?
A: No.

1.13   A Strange Christening

Q: Was this a normal priest conducting a normal christening?
A: Yes.

Q: Was there a good reason for her actions?
A: Yes.

Q: Did she act to protect or help the baby?
A: No.

Q: Did she act to help or protect the priest?
A: Yes.

1.14   Pond Problem

This is so easy that no clue should be needed. However, it can be said that he used no other equipment and no counterbalancing weight. He merely arranged the planks.

1.15   Walking and Running

Q: Did the sportsmen travel in a circle?
A: No. They travelled in a straight line from A to B.

Q: Does this involve going backwards, sideways, up, or down?
A: No.

Q: Did they both travel exactly the same distance?
A: Yes.

Q: Was it a normal bicycle?
A: No.

1.16   Church Bells I

Q: Was it just the sound of the bells which indicated to him that it was a recording?
A: Yes.

Q: Was it to do with the number of times that the bells chimed?
A: No.

Q: Did he hear some additional sound which should not have been there?
A: No.

Q: Was the clue the absence of something which should have been heard?
A: Yes.

1.17 Church Bells II

Q: Did it strike 13 at midday?
A: No. It struck 12.

Q: Was this fault due to the clock mechanism?
A: No.

Q: Was a bird, bat, or insect involved?
A: No.

Q: Was the 13th strike caused by some human action?
A: Yes.

1.18 A Popular Book

Q: Do people read it frequently?
A: Yes.

Q: Do people read it from start to finish?
A: No.

Q: Does it contain a lot of useful information?
A: Yes.

1.19   River Problem I

This is an old chestnut which can be solved by leaving things, taking things, and coming back for things. If you play around with the possibilities you will soon arrive at the answer. When you do, do not relax just yet; the next puzzle will test your mettle.

1.20   River Problem II

This solution requires more lateral thinking than the last puzzle. He made it safely across with all three items. At no time was the fox left alone with the duck or the corn. Nor was the duck left alone with the corn. Yet the boat could contain only the man and one of his charges at any one time.

1.21   River Problem III

The man uses a piece of rope. But how?

1.22   Bill and Ben

Q: Does Bill run exactly as fast as Ben?
A: Yes.

Q: Do they both start in the same place and finish in the same place?
A: Yes.

Q: Does Ben run further than Bill?
A: Yes.

Q: Is the course somehow more difficult for Ben?
A: Yes.

Q: Is it a normal racetrack?
A: No.

1.23 The Missing Brick

Q: In solving this problem, does anything about the house, the brick, the couple, or the other people involved matter?
A: No.

Q: Does what went before this matter?
A: No.

Q: Does what follows this matter?
A: Yes.

1.24 A Strange Flight

Q: Did the duck have the pipe in its mouth?
A: No.

Q: Did the duck have something else in its mouth?
A: Yes.

Q: Does anything about the old man, the old lady, or the plane matter?
A: No.

Q: Does what happened before matter?
A: Yes.

2 Intriguing Puzzles

2.1 Stamp Collection

Q: Did he recognize the collection?
A: Yes.

Q: Was it a genuine stamp collection worth a lot of money?
A: Yes.

Q: Had he previously sold it or given it away?
A: No.

Q: Did he previously own all the stamps which were in this collection?
A: Yes.

Q: So he now had a set of duplicates?
A: No.

2.2 Sheepish Behavior

Q: Did the sheep come onto the road in order to be warmer or better protected than in the fields?
A: No.

Q: Did they come onto the road in order to get away from something in the fields?
A: No.

Q: Was there something which attracted them to the road?
A: Yes.

Q: Does this happen only in very cold weather?
A: Yes.

2.3 The Tennis Match

Q: Did they both use the same court, net, balls, and rackets for the three sets?
A: Yes. Nothing about the environment or equipment changed.

Q: Did Pete's game improve or Jim's deteriorate?
A: Pete's game improved. Jim's play stayed the same.

Q: To an outside observer, would Pete have appeared to have been trying his hardest during the first set?
A: Yes.

Q: Did Pete change something which caused his play to dramatically improve?
A: Yes.

2.4 Surrounded

Q: Had the detectives seen him and were they intent on arresting him?
A: Yes.

Q: Did he escape across the stage?
A: No.

Q: Did he use the audience to help him escape?
A: Yes.

2.5 The Banker

Q: Was Bernard worried about business?
A: No.

Q: Was he worried about his safety?
A: Yes.

Q: Was any kidnapping, robbery, or criminal activity involved or the cause of his worry?
A: No.

Q: Was he normally worried on trains?
A: No. He travelled to work on one every day.

Q: Was anyone with him?
A: Yes. His nephew.

Q: Was the nephew worried?
A: No. He was happy.

2.6 A Curious Place

Q: Is it a town or a building?
A: No.

Q: Is this a real or an imaginary place?
A: A real place.

Q: Is it a pleasant place to be?
A: No.

Q: Is it a dangerous place?
A: Yes (but irrelevant).

Q: Has anyone ever been there for a day?
A: No.

2.7 Grandmother's Letter

Q: Was the stamp or the envelope valuable?
A: No.

Q: Was there something of value in the envelope?
A: Yes.

Q: Was he pleased because he somehow got some money?
A: Yes.

2.8 Theft at the Wedding

Q: Did he somehow manage to get everybody to empty their pockets?
A: No.

Q: Was it anything to do with the contents of the wallet?
A: No.

Q: Did he discover the culprit immediately or sometime later?
A: Sometime later.

2.9 The Free Extension

Q: Did the builder gain some benefit from this whole process?
A: Yes. Definitely.

Q: Were the two men related or was there an existing business relationship between them?
A: No.

Q: Did the man subsequently provide some service, reward, or payment to the builder?
A: No.

Q: Was the man famous?
A: Yes.

2.10 Bridge Crossing

Q: Did they cross at night?
A: No.

Q: Did they use the bridge?
A: No.

Q: Did they swim across?
A: No.

Q: Did they get wet?
A: Yes.

2.11 The Seven-Year Itch

Q: Did the woman wait in order to avoid observation by the police or criminals?
A: No.

Q: Was the money and jewelry stolen?
A: Yes (but irrelevant).

Q: Would she have liked to have spent the money earlier?
A: Yes!

Q: Was she somehow physically prevented from spending the money?
A: Yes.

Q: Was she in prison?
A: No.

2.12 Hit Out

Q: Did the patient have some grievance against the surgeon?
A: No.

Q: Was the surgeon a genuine surgeon who had carried out a proper surgical operation on the patient?
A: Yes.

Q: Does the nature of the operation matter?
A: No.

Q: Does the profession of the patient matter?
A: Yes.

2.13 A Green Wedding

Q: Did the cleric suggest something which would not need to be cleared up?
A: Yes.

Q: Is it something which is non-polluting and disappears in a short time?
A: Yes.

Q: Does it involve water in some form?
A: No.

2.14 Sell the Truth

Q: Does he manufacture something used by people of all ages?
A: Yes.

Q: Is his product in common use?
A: Yes.

Q: Would he sell more if middle-aged people were more honest about their appearance, health, size, or weight?
A: No.

Q: Would he sell more if middle-aged people were more honest about their age?
A: Yes.

2.15 The Dried Peas

Q: Do customers buy the ball containing the dried peas for a specific purpose?
A: Yes.

Q: Do the purchasers play soccer with this ball?
A: Yes.

Q: Do they keep the peas inside the ball, or take them out?
A: The peas stay inside the ball.

Q: Do they play a special game with this ball?
A: No. They play regular soccer as well as they can.

2.16 The Dog That Did Not Die

Q: Was the girl's dog unharmed throughout?
A: Yes.

Q: Had the mother been misinformed?
A: No.

Q: Did the mother deliberately lie to her daughter?
A: Yes.

Q: Did she do this out of spite or malice, or to punish or threaten her daughter?
A: No.

Q: Did she do this for a particular reason and was she successful in her aim?
A: Yes.

2.17   High Office

Q: Was Tom chosen for a specific reason?
A: Yes.

Q: Does Tom have some particular skill or aptitude?
A: No.

Q: Could anyone be given this job?
A: No.

Q: Was the previous holder of the job able to read, write, etc.?
A: Yes, he was very accomplished.

2.18   The Follower

Q: Was he a danger to her?
A: No.

Q: Was he trying to help her?
A: Yes.

Q: Had he seen something wrong with her car?
A: No.

2.19   Money to Burn

Q: Does this involve some kind of insurance claim?
A: No.

Q: Did the robber know what was in the bag?
A: Yes.

Q: Was the messenger part of the plot?

A: No. He was honest.

Q: Was the money genuine?
A: No. It was counterfeit.

2.20   Not a Kidnapper

Q: Was the banker able to give any clue about the kidnapper?
A: No.

Q: Did the suspect have a physical or mental disability?
A: No.

Q: Did he have some trait or characteristic which indicated that he had not committed this crime?
A: Yes.

Q: Was it something you would immediately see or hear or recognize if you met him?
A: No.

Q: Was it something which you would recognize if you watched him over a period of time?
A: Yes.

2.21   Ruination

Q: Did the employee save the company from some disaster or major cost?
A: No.

Q: Was the employee rewarded or punished?
A: Rewarded.

Q: Was it an accident?
A: Yes.

Q: Was the ruined output somehow more valuable?
A: Yes.

Q: What sort of products did the factory produce?
A: Paper.

2.22 The Bet

Q: Did he actually have a letter transported that distance in 45 minutes?
A: Yes.

Q: Did he use cannons, guns, gunpowder, or explosives?
A: No.

Q: Was the starting point somewhere unusual, such as the top of a mountain or cliff?
A: No. His method would work in any open country.

Q: Did he use horses or some other running animal?
A: No.

Q: Did his method involve considerable preparation and help?
A: Yes.

2.23 Days Off

Q: Did the employees deliberately collaborate in order for each to have a day off?
A: No.

Q: Was there some connection or association between the employees other than their work?
A: No.

Q: Did each one always take the same day of the week off?
A: Yes.

Q: Does the type or place of work matter?
A: No.

Q: Were they similar in culture or nationality?
A: No. They were quite different.

2.24 An Irish Puzzle

Q: Did the man at the garage know Milligan personally or have any connection with him?
A: No.

Q: Did Milligan ever drive anybody anywhere?
A: No.

Q: Was the eagle a genuine eagle?
A: Yes.

Q: Was it alive?
A: No.

Q: Is Milligan's profession important?
A: Yes.

3 Grisly Puzzles

3.1 A Shocking Discovery

Q: Had he been deceived and robbed?
A: Yes.

Q: Was anything missing from his wallet or pockets, or his jewelry or clothes?
A: No.

Q: Did he find something new which gave him the shock?
A: Yes.

Q: Was it on his body?
A: Yes.

3.2 Clean Sweep

Q: Was her cleaning job in a shop, office, school, or factory?
A: No.

Q: Was her fainting caused by something she saw?
A: Yes.

Q: Was it a body or part of a body?
A: Yes.

Q: Was it a surprise for her to see a body?
A: No.

3.3 Death on the Boat

Q: Was his death an accident?
A: Yes.

Q: Was anyone else on the boat at the time of his death?
A: No.

Q: Had he been hit by anything on or part of the boat?
A: No.

Q: Was any bird, fish, or marine mammal involved?
A: No.

Q: Had he been hit by something which fell out of the sky?
A: Yes.

3.4 A Rum Find

Q: Was the rum poisoned in some way?
A: No.

Q: Was it genuine rum?
A: Yes.

Q: Did the cask contain something other than the rum?
A: Yes.

3.5 Broken Match

Q: Was the match instrumental in the man's death?
A: Yes.

Q: Was he trying to light something with the match prior to his death?
A: No.

Q: Was he alone in the field?
A: Yes.

Q: Did he know he was going to die before he entered the field?
A: Yes.

Q: Was he murdered?
A: No.

Q: Did he fall into the field?
A: Yes.

3.6   The Cut Finger

Q: Was the cut healed?
A: No.

Q: Did he put his hand into a sink or a bowl?
A: No.

Q: Was he outdoors when this happened?
A: Yes.

Q: Was he pleased when he drew his hand out of the water?
A: No.

3.7   The Music Stopped

Q: Did she die because the music stopped?
A: Yes.

Q: Was the music some kind of signal?
A: Yes.

Q: Was she doing something dangerous?
A: Yes.

Q: Was it some kind of entertainment?
A: Yes.

3.8   The Dog Choker

Q: Was the dog a guard dog?
A: Yes.

Q: Had the vet found evidence of poison or gas?
A: No.

Q: Had the vet deduced that there was a danger in the house?
A: Yes.

Q: Had the vet discovered what it was the dog was choking on?
A: Yes.

3.9   The Movie

Q: Were they in a normal cinema?
A: Yes.

Q: Did any of the other people there notice the murder?
A: Yes. Everyone did.

Q: Did the police release Tom because he was innocent of any crime?
A: Yes.

Q: Did Tom shoot Joe in self-defense?
A: No.

Q: Were the people who restrained Tom angry with him?
A: No.

3.10   The Damaged Car

Q: Did he do this to claim on insurance?
A: No.

Q: Did he deliberately and voluntarily damage his own car?
A: Yes.

Q: Was there a monetary reason for doing this?
A: No.

Q: Did he set out that day intending to damage his car?
A: No.

Q: Did something happen which caused him to damage his car?
A: Yes.

Q: Did he do it because he wanted to avoid some worse consequence?
A: Yes.

3.11 The Motorcyclist

Q: Was the man trying to injure or kill himself?
A: No.

Q: Did he know the motorcyclist who hit him?
A: No.

Q: Did he expect the motorcyclist to stop?
A: Yes.

Q: Was the motorcyclist expecting the man to step out in front of him?
A: No.

Q: Did the man's profession have something to do with motorcycling?
A: Yes.

3.12 Swimmer in the Forest

Q: Did he die at the spot where he was found?
A: Yes.

Q: Had he previously been swimming?
A: Yes.

Q: Was he taken to the forest against his will?
A: Yes.

Q: Was he taken deliberately?
A: No, accidentally.

3.13 The Dark Room

Q: Would the man have been shot if he had not entered the dark room?

A: No.

Q: Did he do something in the dark room which directly led to his being shot?

A: Yes.

Q: Did this happen during a war?

A: It could have happened in peacetime or war but is more likely during a war.

Q: Were either of the men in uniform?

A: No.

3.14 The Two Vans

Q: Can we consider the vans, their situations, and the fitness and skills of the drivers to be identical at the time of this accident?

A: Yes.

Q: Was one able to open a door and escape and the other not?

A: Yes.

Q: Did one of them do something different (and smarter) than the other?

A: Yes.

Q: If they had been driving cars rather than vans would the outcome have been different?

A: Yes. They would probably both have drowned.

3.15 Suicide

Q: Did some noise or action wake him?

A: No. He awoke naturally.

Q: Did he commit suicide because something happened which caused him to realize something?
A: Yes.

Q: Did he see something which caused the realization?
A: No.

Q: Did he hear something which caused the realization?
A: Yes.

Q: Was there anyone else in the house?
A: No.

Q: Was it a special kind of house?
A: Yes.

3.16   The Plane Crash

Q: Was the news flash a genuine one or was it part of the movie?
A: It was a genuine news flash.

Q: Was the news flash accurate: had the plane crashed with no survivors?
A: Yes.

Q: Had the woman's husband got off the flight before it left?
A: No.

Q: Had she planned the plane crash or did she know it would happen?
A: No.

Q: Did she know that her husband had not been killed?
A: Yes.

3.17   One Beautiful Morning

Q: Did the man see something unusual, terrible, or frightening from the window?
A: No.

Q: Did he commit suicide because it was a beautiful morning?
A: Yes.

Q: Had he done something terrible which he now regretted?
A: Yes.

Q: Is his profession important?
A: Yes. He was a preacher.

3.18   The Blanket Mystery

Q: Did the man inadvertently cause an accident?
A: No.

Q: Did he somehow deliberately cause the deaths of the people?
A: He deliberately caused their deaths.

Q: Did he kill them or did he have accomplices who killed them?
A: His accomplices killed them.

Q: Were the people who died travelling when this happened?
A: Yes.

Q: Could this have happened recently?
A: No. It happened during the nineteenth century.

3.19   The Deadly Bite

Q: Did she know it was dangerous?
A: Yes.

Q: Did the man know it was dangerous?
A: Yes.

Q: Did the food contain some medical or physical danger?
A: No.

Q: Did he die soon afterwards?
A: No. He died many years afterwards.

Q: What kind of food was it?
A: Fruit.

3.20 Bad Boy

Q: Did the boy take some deliberate action which resulted in the man's death?
A: Yes.

Q: Does this involve firearms, electricity, or water?
A: No.

Q: Did the boy mean to kill the man?
A: No.

Q: Did the boy enter the house or put something into the house?
A: No.

4 Diabolical Puzzles

4.1 The Nursery Rhyme

Q: Did the baby do something on him?
A: No. The baby was as good as gold.

Q: Was the choice of nursery rhyme inappropriate?
A: Yes, very.

Q: Did he discover something about the baby in the course
of reciting the rhyme?
A: Yes.

4.2 The Elder Twin

Q: Were Kerry and Terry genuine human twins, born of
the same mother of the same pregnancy?
A: Yes.

Q: Was Terry, the older twin, born before Kerry?
A: Yes.

Q: Was her birthday always before his?
A: Yes.

Q: Does where the births took place matter?
A: Yes.

4.3 Fair Shares

Q: Does the solution involve weighing or measuring?
A: No.

Q: Does the solution involve cutting the cake and letting
people choose?
A: Yes.

Q: Is the cake cut one piece at a time?
A: Yes.

Q: Is the system fair—that is, no one can complain that someone else has received too large a piece or that they themselves have received too small a piece?
A: Yes.

4.4   The Sealed Envelope

Q: Did the wife somehow open and then re-seal the envelope?
A: No.

Q: Did she replace the original envelope with another?
A: No.

Q: Can this be done with an ordinary envelope and letter?
A: Generally speaking, yes it can; but not always.

Q: Did she use some kind of tool?
A: Yes. A kind of needle.

4.5   Tattoo

Q: Were they trying to identify themselves in some way?
A: No.

Q: Did they share a common occupation?
A: Yes.

Q: Does where they were tattooed matter?
A: Yes, it was on their backs.

Q: Did this happen recently?
A: No, about two centuries ago.

4.6   Suitcase for Hire

Q: Was the shop a rental-only shop?
A: No.

Q: Did most customers at this shop choose to rent their suitcases rather than buy them?

A: Yes.

Q: Did this have anything to do with price, or insurance, or choice of style?
A: No.

Q: Did people rent because of convenience?
A: Yes.

Q: Was Pat in the United States?
A: No.

4.7 The Tennis Tournament

There is a simple, logical, and lateral way of working out the number of matches in such a knockout tournament whatever the number of entries. Try thinking in terms of winners and losers.

4.8 The Key

Q: Was this a regular man in a regular house with a regular key?
A: Yes.

Q: Did he put the key in the bucket of water to prevent some person or some creature getting it?
A: No.

Q: Does this involve criminal intent or the prevention of criminal action?
A: No.

Q: Did he do this to protect the safety of himself or his wife?
A: Yes.

Q: Was it to protect against a likely accident?
A: Yes.

4.9   That's Fast!

Q: Does this involve gases, atoms, or tiny particles?
A: No.

Q: Did Harry have special equipment or skills?
A: No. Anyone can do this.

Q: Did he intend to do this?
A: No.

Q: Did whatever travelled at that high speed make a very loud noise?
A: It made a noise, but not a very loud noise.

Q: Did it travel very far?
A: No, only about two feet.

4.10   A Man in a Bar

Q: Did the two men know each other?
A: No.

Q: Was the man thirsty?
A: No.

Q: Did he really want the drink?
A: Yes.

Q: Was it some kind of signal or message?
A: No.

Q: What kind of drink was it?
A: Wine.

4.11   The 88 Hours

Q: Did he sit still voluntarily?
A: No. He sat down voluntarily but thereafter he would have preferred to get up.

Q: Was he physically restrained in the chair?
A: Yes.

Q: Does this involve any criminal intent?
A: No.

Q: Was he rewarded for sitting still for so long?
A: No.

Q: Was he in good health when he sat down?
A: No. He had a bad toothache.

4.12 Sand Trap

Q: Were the cars stolen?
A: No. He had bought them legitimately.

Q: Did he bury them to make some financial gain?
A: Yes.

Q: Did he intend that they be dug up later when something had changed?
A: Yes.

Q: Was he taking advantage of unusual circumstances?
A: Yes.

4.13 Building Demolition

Q: Did the original building have some flaw or defect which made it necessary for it to be replaced?
A: No.

Q: Was the new building significantly better in some way?
A: No.

Q: Were both new and old buildings used for the same purpose?
A: Yes.

Q: Is that purpose relevant to the solution of this puzzle?
A: Yes.

Q: Did the building contain something of value?
A: Yes.

4.14 The Torn Cheque

Q: Is the number 217 relevant?
A: Yes.

Q: Is he sending the cheque to his ex-wife or to anyone he knows personally?
A: No.

Q: Is the cheque for the taxman or some other official?
A: No.

Q: Does the recipient of the cheque like puzzles?
A: No.

Q: Is he angry with the person to whom he is sending the cheque?
A: Yes.

4.15 The Weather Report

Q: Is it possible to deduce where this is from the information given?
A: Yes.

Q: Did the weather report give any other details?
A: No.

Q: Did the weather report state whether the temperature was in degrees Fahrenheit or Celsius?
A: No.

4.16 Odd Animals

These animals all have something quite specific in common. However, it has nothing to do with habitat, food-stuffs, appearance, activity, procreation, zoos, or physical attributes. What can it be?

4.17 The Shorter Program

Q: Was this a live concert which finished early?
A: No. It was recorded.

Q: Did the program producer or presenter make a mistake?
A: Yes.

Q: Did they play all of the music they intended to play?
A: Yes.

Q: Was the music on tape or compact disc?
A: No.

4.18   Traffic Trouble

Q: Did the change in traffic regulations mean that more cars passed the area where the sex shops were located?
A: No.

Q: Did the change in regulations cause a change in people's sexual behavior?
A: No.

Q: Did the change in regulations have to do with speeding or parking?
A: No.

Q: Did people buy something from the sex shops which helped them to comply with or evade the new regulations?
A: Yes.

4.19   Blackmail

Q: Did the criminal send an invoice to someone who had not died?
A: No.

Q: Did he send an invoice to someone who was above suspicion of ordering pornographic books?
A: Yes.

Q: Was this because of the dead man's character or profession?
A: No.

4.20   A Good Night's Sleep

Q: Was it a normal hotel?
A: Yes.

Q: Were the drapes normal curtains, used to exclude light at the window?
A: Yes.

Q: Was sound or light stopping him from getting to sleep?
A: No.

Q: Was there something abnormal about the man?
A: Yes.

Q: Was it nighttime?
A: Yes.

Q: Was anyone else involved?
A: No.

4.21   Grateful for Poor Service

Q: Was it a dangerous item which was for sale?
A: No.

Q: Was it a service rather than a product?
A: Yes.

Q: Was there anything about the man which made it wrong or inappropriate for him to use this service?
A: No.

Q: Was the official acting correctly or in the man's best interests?
A: No.

Q: When did this happen?
A: In 1912.

4.22   Free T-shirts

Q: Did ordering and receiving the T-shirt damage his

health in some way?
A: No.

Q: Did it result in financial loss?
A: Yes.

Q: Was the T-shirt offer some kind of scam by criminals?
A: No.

Q: Was the T-shirt offer a genuine offer?
A: No. It had some ulterior purpose.

Q: Was the T-shirt harmless?
A: Yes.

Q: Was the man himself breaking the law?
A: Yes.

Q: Was his name on a wanted list?
A: No.

4.23   Bank Robbery I

Q: Did the bank employee alert the police?
A: Not immediately. He did something more important first.

Q: Did the gang get out of the bank?
A: Yes.

Q: Did they get into their getaway car?
A: No.

Q: Could this have happened in any bank?
A: No.

4.24   Bank Robbery II

Q: Were the robbers frustrated because they could not spend or convert the money they had stolen?
A: Yes.

Q: Did they steal valid currency which could be spent?
A: Yes.

Q: Did they steal numbered or marked notes which could be traced?
A: No.

Q: Could they deposit their loot in other banks?
A: Yes, but that would have given them away.

4.25 A Puzzling Attack

Q: Were any of the four criminals?
A: No.

Q: Did the three have a sound reason for beating up the fourth?
A: Yes. A very sound reason.

Q: Had he said something which inflamed them?
A: Yes.

Q: Were any dwarfs, lighthouse-keepers, or blocks of ice involved?
A: No.

THE ANSWERS

1 Tempting Puzzles

1.1 A Fishy Tale

The vet could see that the goldfish was dying of old age so to spare the old lady's feelings he dashed out and bought a young but identical fish and disposed of the old one.

1.2 The Lost Passenger

Little Billy, as his name suggests, was a goat who unfortunately ate his label, so no one knew where he was supposed to go!

1.3 The Book

She was returning an overdue library book.

1.4 A Hairy Problem

The hair on a man's head is usually at least twenty years older than the hair in his moustache. (This solution is not guaranteed to be biologically correct but it does have an inherent plausibility.)

1.5 The Birds

They were two golfers. In golf parlance, one had hit a "birdie" (one under par) and the other an "eagle" (two under par).

1.6 Blinded at Teatime

He had left his teaspoon in his cup of tea. When he raised the cup to drink, the teaspoon handle poked him in the eye, temporarily blinding him.

1.7 Countdown

The man was counting the pins as he removed them from a new shirt. Unfortunately, he missed one.

1.8 Weather Forecast

In 72 hours it would be midnight again, so it could not be "bright and sunny."

1.9 No West

At the exact center of the earth it is impossible to look east or west but you could look north or south.

1.10 The Blind Beggar

The blind beggar was the sister of her brother who died.

1.11 The Truck Driver

The truck driver was walking.

1.12 Mountains Ahead

The plane is sitting on the ground at the airport in Denver, Colorado.

1.13   A Strange Christening

The priest's surplice had caught fire from one of the candles.

1.14   Pond Problem

He lays the planks as shown in this diagram.

1.15   Walking and Running

The two keen sportsmen started at their fitness club, one on the cycling machine and the other on the walking machine. After half an hour of indoor exercise they went for a run. The distance from A to B is 2 miles.

1.16   Church Bells I

The final chime ended abruptly and without the reverberation of the other chimes.

1.17   Church Bells II

There was a joker living in a nearby house. Each night, using his rifle and a silencer, he fired a bullet at the bell after the twelfth stroke.

1.18 A Popular Book

The book is a telephone directory.

1.19 River Problem I

First the man took the duck across, then he came back and took the fox over. He left the fox on the far side of the river and returned with the duck. He then left the duck on the near side and took the corn over. Then he returned and took the duck across. Pretty straightforward, eh?

1.20 River Problem II

The man tied the duck to the back of the boat with a rope. The duck swam along behind the boat as the man ferried the fox and corn over in turn.

1.21 River Problem III

He stretches a long rope from point A to point B as shown.

1.22 Bill and Ben

Bill and Ben are laboratory rats. Bill has run through a certain maze many times and has learned to complete it quickly. When Ben is introduced to the course for the first time, it takes him ten times as long.

1.23 The Missing Brick

A duck grabbed the brick in its mouth and flew off with it!

1.24 A Strange Flight

The duck had a brick in its mouth (see previous puzzle)!

This and the puzzle before it are reciprocal puzzles—each holds the solution to the other.

2 Intriguing Puzzles

2.1   Stamp Collection

The man had recently left his wife to live with his mistress. The angry wife had advertised the man's prized stamp collection for sale, so he quickly bought his own stamps to stop anyone else doing so.

2.2   Sheepish Behavior

The sheep kept coming to the road because they liked to eat the salt put on the road to stop it freezing.

2.3   The Tennis Match

Pete could play tennis with either hand but he was better as a left-hander. He started off playing right-handed but switched after the first set.

2.4   Surrounded

The fugitive leapt up and shouted, "Fire, fire!" Pandemonium broke out and the audience all rushed for the exits. He easily escaped in the confusion.

2.5   The Banker

The train was a roller-coaster. The banker had promised to take his nephew for a ride but hated the experience. He was relieved it was over.

2.6   A Curious Place

The place is Venus, where a day is longer than a year.

Venus takes 225 Earth days to go around the sun but it takes 243 Earth days to rotate on its axis. In any event, it is unlikely that many people would like to go there for either period; the average temperature is around 885°F (460°C), the pressure is about 94 atmospheres, and there are thick clouds of sulphuric acid!

2.7 Grandmother's Letter

The boy's grandmother was Queen Victoria. In this true incident the boy sold the letter for five pounds sterling (over $20 in those days).

2.8 Theft at the Wedding

Two weeks later, when the couple returned from their honeymoon, the whole family sat down to watch the video of the wedding. They were horrified to see, caught on the camera, the groom going through his father-in-law's pockets and stealing his wallet.

2.9 The Free Extension

It is a true story and the man was Picasso. The builder wisely decided that by building the extension he would be able to retain Picasso's rough sketch of the plans, which would be worth far more than the cost of the construction work. He was right.

2.10 Bridge Crossing

They spread out and waded across the river, which was only six inches deep.

2.11 The Seven-Year Itch

The woman had been shipwrecked. She found a pirate's treasure but was not rescued for seven years.

2.12 Hit Out

The patient is a boxer. The last thing he heard was the anesthetist counting 1, 2, 3, 4, and as he comes round he automatically tries to beat the count and resume the fight against his opponent.

2.13 A Green Wedding

The cleric suggested that people throw colored birdseed.

2.14 Sell the Truth

He made the candles that go on birthday cakes.

2.15 The Dried Peas

The dried peas are inside soccer balls for the use of blind people, to enable them to hear the ball.

2.16 The Dog That Did Not Die

This story reportedly concerns the youthful Shirley Temple. Her mother told her the lie that her pet dog had been killed in order to induce real sadness and tears for a movie scene which was about to be filmed.

2.17 High Office

Tom is an infant who is crown prince of his country. Tom's father, the king, has just died leaving a very inexperienced new head of state.

2.18 The Follower

He had seen a man hide in the back of the woman's car as she paid at the gasoline station. He followed her to warn her and was pleased to see her pull into the police station.

2.19 Money to Burn

The robber's mother was a widow who owed the bank $100,000. The bank had threatened to repossess her house so her son devised a plan. He forged $100,000 and she gave it to the bank messenger, who signed for it. The forgeries were good enough to fool the messenger but would never fool the bank so the son had to rob the messenger before he got back to the bank.

2.20 Not a Kidnapper

The inspector noticed that the man wrote with his left hand. He asked him to tie a knot. The man was left-handed and tied a left-handed knot. The knots tied around the hands and feet of the victim were right-handed knots.

2.21 Ruination

The employee discovered an important new product. He left out a primary ingredient in the batch of paper he was making. He was thus responsible for accidentally producing the first blotting paper!

2.22 The Bet

He tied the letter inside a hollowed-out cricket ball (which is about the same size as a baseball). He then had it thrown from man to man with the men standing about 60 yards (55 metres) apart along the entire way.

2.23 Days Off

All seven employees were very religious and they all had different Sabbaths. The Christian took off on Sunday, the Greek Monday, the Persian Tuesday, the Assyrian Wednesday, the Egyptian Thursday, the Arabian Muslim Friday, and the Jew Saturday.

2.24 An Irish Puzzle

Milligan stuffed animals. The man in the garage had heard that Milligan was a famous local taxidermist and thought that he ran some kind of taxi service!

3 Grisly Puzzles

3.1 A Shocking Discovery

He had a pain in his back and when he felt it he found a recently stitched incision. The woman was a lure for a crooked surgeon who removed healthy human organs and sold them to rich people needing organ transplants. On examination by X-ray the man found that one of his kidneys was gone!

3.2 Clean Sweep

The woman works at a teaching hospital as an orderly. It is her job to clean bodies and get them ready for student lectures. She collapses when she sees that the body awaiting her is the body of her brother, who had earlier died in an accident. She did not know that he had left his body to science.

3.3 Death on the Boat

He had been hit by a block of frozen toilet waste ejected by a passenger jet high above him. It fell into the sea leaving no trace.

3.4 A Rum Find

When they finished the rum they broke open the cask to find a body inside. In the eighteenth and nineteenth centuries, bodies were often shipped back to England from Jamaica this way. (British admiral Horatio Nelson's body was reputedly brought home to England in a barrel of rum after the battle of Trafalgar.)

3.5 Broken Match

He and a number of other passengers were making a balloon trip in a desperate attempt to escape from a country. The balloon had to lose weight to stop it from crashing. He drew the short match and had to jump.

3.6 The Cut Finger

This incident took place in South America. The unfortunate man was camping by a river. When he put his hand in the river the blood attracted piranha fish, which removed his finger including the cut!

3.7 The Music Stopped

She was a circus tightrope walker. Her most daring act was to cross a high wire while blindfolded. The band played while she crossed and when the music stopped it was the signal that she had reached the end of the wire and could safely alight. Unfortunately, one day the conductor was taken ill at the last minute and the stand-in conductor, unaware of the importance of the timing, ended the music just a little too soon. She stepped off the wire to her death.

3.8 The Dog Choker

The vet found two human fingers in the dog's throat. They belonged to a burglar. The vet feared that the burglar was still in the house, afraid of the dog and hiding in a closet.

3.9 The Movie

Tom and Joe were the stars of the movie. Tom shot Joe in a sequence in the movie. When Tom left he was mobbed by fans seeking his autograph.

3.10 The Damaged Car

A few minutes earlier, the man had been the driver in a fatal hit-and-run accident. He drove to the isolated area and made it look as though the car had been stolen and vandalized. He then phoned the police to report his car stolen. (This is a true incident. He was later caught and sent to prison.)

3.11 The Motorcyclist

The man was an examiner testing a motorcyclist. He instructed the motorcyclist to go round the block and then to do an emergency stop when the examiner stepped out from the sidewalk. Unfortunately, another motorcyclist of similar appearance came by first. Knowing nothing of the arrangement, he hit the examiner.

3.12 Swimmer in the Forest

During a forest fire some months earlier, a fire-fighting plane had scooped up water from the lake to drop on the fire. The plane had accidentally picked up the unfortunate swimmer.

3.13 The Dark Room

The man was a secret service agent who had recently killed several enemy agents. He entered a confessional in a church and confessed to the killings. However, he was under suspicion and had been followed. The man he confessed to was not a priest but an enemy agent who had seen him enter the church.

3.14 The Two Vans

One man tried to open the front door of his van but could not because of the water pressure. The other man climbed into the back of the van, easily opened the sliding door, and thereby escaped.

3.15 Suicide

The man is a lighthouse-keeper. He woke up in the darkness with a nagging feeling that he had forgotten something. He turned on the radio and heard a report that a ship had crashed onto rocks with great loss of life. He realized that it happened because he forgot to start the light that night.

3.16 The Plane Crash

The movie had been shown a week earlier. Susan had taped it then on her videocassette recorder to watch that evening.

3.17 One Beautiful Morning

The man was the leader of a religious cult. Believing that the world would end that night he had offered his followers the choice of taking poison or seeing the destruction of the world. Many, including his own children, had chosen poison. He and others had gone to sleep expecting to wake to Armageddon. When the next day dawned as a beautiful summer morning he knew that he had made a terrible mistake.

3.18 The Blanket Mystery

He was an Indian brave who sent smoke signals alerting a war party to the approach of a cavalry troop.

3.19 The Deadly Bite

The woman was Eve, who gave Adam the forbidden fruit from the tree in the Garden of Eden. By breaking God's instruction, Adam became mortal and died.

3.20 The Bad Boy

Out of mischief, the boy climbed onto the roof of the man's house and placed a plank of wood over the chimney. The man, who had been asleep in his parlor, was suffocated by fumes from his fire.

4 Diabolical Puzzles

4.1 The Nursery Rhyme

The man recites the nursery rhyme "This little piggy went to market, this little piggy stayed home . . ." while wiggling each of the baby's toes. But there is one toe too many! To his embarrassment, he finds that the baby has six toes on one foot.

4.2 The Elder Twin

At the time she went into labor, the twins' mother was travelling from Guam to Hawaii. The older twin, Terry, was born on March 1st. Shortly afterwards, the mother crossed the International Date Line and Kerry, the younger twin, was born. The date was February 28th. In leap years, the younger twin celebrates her birthday two days before the older twin, since February 28 is two days before March 1st.

4.3 Fair Shares

Suppose there are a number of people. Pick one person, A, by lot if necessary. Ask A to cut a piece of the cake that he would be happy with as his share. Now go round the group. If B objects then ask B to cut a bit off A's piece so that he (B) would be happy to take what remains. If B does not object ask C and so on. If nobody objects, then let A have that piece. Continuing this process will give a division which satisfies everybody.

4.4   The Sealed Envelope

There is usually a small gap at the top of the envelope where the flap has been folded over. The wife inserted a knitting needle through the gap and under the fold of the letter. By rotating the needle she wound the letter tightly around it. She then removed it, read the letter, and replaced it using the actions in reverse.

4.5   Tattoo

The men were sailors, who were often flogged for minor offenses on board ship. Some captains refused to whip a man's back if it carried the image of Christ.

4.6   Suitcase for Hire

Pat was a Westerner in Tokyo. Houses there are small and, in order to save space, people tend to rent any large item which they might use only occasionally. Most Japanese rent the suitcases they take on holiday.

4.7   The Tennis Tournament

The answer is 212 matches including the final. There is a very easy way to solve this seemingly difficult problem. Each match must produce one winner and one loser. Everyone except the tournament winner loses exactly once, so the number of matches is exactly the same as the number of losers. So to have 212 losers there must be exactly 212 matches.

4.8 The Key

The man's wife was an habitual sleepwalker. She had previously opened the front door in her sleep and walked out into the road. He placed the key in the bucket of cold water so that, if she reached into the water to get it, the cold sensation would waken her.

4.9 That's Fast!

Harry broke a pane of glass. A crack in glass starts in one place and travels across the glass at a speed of over 3000 miles (4800 kilometres) per hour.

4.10 A Man in a Bar

The man was a priest conducting a communion service in a nearby church when they ran short of altar wine. Only red wine would do.

4.11 The 88 Hours

The man had a nasty toothache and he went to the dentist at 5 P.M. on a Friday evening. The dentist's assistants, including the anesthetist, had all gone and the dentist could not administer an anesthetic. The man insisted that the dentist should operate even without anesthetic so the dentist said that he would have to strap the man into the chair. This was done. The dentist then suffered a heart attack and died. The poor man was left strapped in the chair and unable to move. It was a holiday weekend and no staff reported for work until 9 A.M. on the following Tuesday morning—88 hours later.

4.12 Sand Trap

This incident reputedly occurred during the war between Israel and Egypt. Because of import duties, Mercedes cars were much more expensive in Egypt than in Israel. When Israel seized vast tracts of the Sinai desert, a clever Israeli businessman realized that the land would have to be handed back to Egypt after the war. By burying the cars he effectively exported them when the border shifted without them actually moving! His Egyptian associate subsequently sold them at a handsome profit.

4.13 Building Demolition

The building was the Australian National Mint. Over many years, so much gold dust had been absorbed into the fabric of the building that it was well worthwhile to demolish the building, extract the gold, and rebuild.

4.14 The Torn Cheque

The man had ordered a bicycle for his son as a gift. The advertisement had not stated that it came in 217 pieces as a self-assembly kit. This was his revenge.

4.15 The Weather Report

Since the weather report did not specify degrees in Fahrenheit or Celsius/centigrade, the temperature must have been the same in both scales. Only a temperature of -40 degrees is the same in both Fahrenheit and Celsius/centigrade. That temperature for June would certainly make the place Antarctica.

4.16 Odd Animals

They are all impostors:
The koala bear is not a bear; it is a marsupial.
The prairie dog is not a dog; it is a rodent.
The firefly is not a fly; it is a beetle.

The silkworm is not a worm; it is a caterpillar.
The jackrabbit is not a rabbit; it is a hare.
The guinea pig is not a pig; it is a rodent (and it is not from Guinea, but from South America).

4.17   The Shorter Program

It was a program of contemporary classical music played from a record. The record was played at the wrong speed—45 rpm instead of 33 rpm. Because of the esoteric nature of the composition, this mistake was not noticed until the end of the transmission. It can easily be calculated that the program should have lasted thirty minutes.

4.18   Traffic Trouble

A new traffic regulation, designed to encourage car sharing, stated that only cars carrying two or more passengers could use certain lanes of the freeway. This led to motorists buying blow-up dolls to give the appearance that they were carrying passengers!

4.19   Blackmail

The criminal sent an invoice to a blind man who had recently died. His widow immediately knew that it must be a scam.

4.20   A Good Night's Sleep

The man was deaf. He had to get up early for an important meeting and he was so worried about oversleeping that he could not get to sleep. After opening the curtains, however, he knew that the sunlight would wake him up, so he was no longer worried and fell asleep easily.

4.21 Grateful for Poor Service

The man wanted to buy a first-class ticket on the maiden voyage of the luxury liner *Titanic* in 1912. He was refused because he was black. The *Titanic* sank with great loss of life.

4.22 Free T-shirts

This is a true story from Connecticut. The advertisement was a trap for people who used illegal devices to tap into cable television circuits without paying. It was placed by the owners of the cable television network and could be seen only by people using illegal decoders.The "free" T-shirt was soon followed by a letter informing them that they were committing a federal crime and imposing a $2000 fine. The recipients had little choice but to pay up.

4.23 Bank Robbery I

The bank was on the sixth floor of a tall building. The staff member who struggled free pressed a security button which froze all the elevators. The gang was trapped inside the elevator until the police came to arrest them.

4.24 Bank Robbery II

The robbers discovered to their horror that the currency consisted only of freshly minted coins. All shops and banks were alerted to watch out for anyone trying to exchange large amounts of coin, so the gang was reduced to playing slot machines!

4.25 A Puzzling Attack

They had been trying to solve a lateral thinking problem— this one in fact. When the one posing the problem revealed the answer the others beat him up. (In setting this puzzle, always describe the group and the problem poser in terms of the number of men and women in your own group.)

About the Authors

Paul Sloane was born in Scotland and grew up near Blackpool in the north of England. He studied engineering at Trinity Hall, Cambridge, and graduated with a first-class honors degree. While at Cambridge he met his wife, who is a teacher. They live in Camberley, England, with their three daughters.

Most of Paul Sloane's career has been in the computer industry and he is currently the European vice-president for a software company. He has always been an avid collector and creator of puzzles. His first book, *Lateral Thinking Puzzlers*, was published by Sterling in 1991. Paul Sloane has given speeches and radio talks on the topic of change management and lateral thinking.

Des MacHale was born in County Mayo, Ireland, and is Associate Professor of Mathematics at University College in Cork. He was educated at University College, Galway, and the University of Keele in England. He and his wife, Anne, have five children.

The author of over thirty books, mostly of humor but also one on giving up smoking, Des MacHale has many interests including puzzles, geology, writing, broadcasting, films, photography, numismatics, and, of course, mathematics. He is currently working on three more books.

This is the second book co-authored by Paul Sloane and Des MacHale. It follows on the success of their first book, *Challenging Lateral Thinking Puzzles*, also published by Sterling.

INDEX

Page key: **puzzle,** *clue,* solution